OUTSIDE, LOOKING IN.....

Finding light: My Journey
Through Mental Health Struggles

L J Howells

Grosvenor House
Publishing Limited

This book is published by
Grosvenor House Publishing Ltd
Link House
140 The Broadway, Tolworth, Surrey, KT6 7HT.
www.grosvenorhousepublishing.co.uk

A CIP record for this book
is available from the British Library

Paperback ISBN 978-1-83615-511-9

Thank you to my beautiful wife,
son and family – for keeping me (almost) sane!

Contents

Introduction   1

Chapter 1 – My Family   3

Chapter 2 – My Wider Family   7

Chapter 3 – Happy Memories   11

Chapter 4 – Daily Life   17

Chapter 5 – Fun Times & Hobbies   21

Chapter 6 – Family Holidays   25

Chapter 7 – My Favourite Time Of Year   29

Chapter 8 – School Days   31

Chapter 9 – Transitioning To Comprehensive
            School   35

Chapter 10 – Becoming A Teenager   39

Chapter 11 – Losing Control   45

Chapter 12 – A Hard Lesson To Learn   49

Chapter 13 – Maintaining Balance   53

Chapter 14 – Life Beyond The Classroom   59

Chapter 15 – Moving Away   61

Chapter 16 – Becoming A 'Real' Adult   65

Chapter 17 – Increasing Debt   71

Chapter 18 – As Useful As A One-Handed Clap… 75

Chapter 19 – Escaping Debt & Health Worries 79

Chapter 20 – Searching For The Right Job
          (And Finding My Wife On The Way) 83

Chapter 21 – More Surgery   87

Chapter 22 – A New Beginning   91

Afterword – Looking Forward   93

About the Author   95

Introduction

This is my story and how mental health issues have played a part in important stages of my life. Some people don't believe these issues exist, and others prefer not to acknowledge its existence at all!

I had a happy childhood and a very supportive, loving family – without whom I may well have lost my way. I want to address the myths about mental health issues that allege 'it must be because of how someone was brought up' or 'they couldn't have been shown enough love'. I find these assumptions insulting and stereotypical of an ignorant person who does not want to take the time to truly understand others. I believe some people find it easier to ignore its existence altogether, so it doesn't rear its ugly head in their own lives or affect their immediate social bubbles!

I am by no means suggesting that all mental health issues are the same. I am simply telling you my story to describe how these issues changed me and the world around me.

I was outside, looking in.

Chapter 1

My Family

I am extremely lucky to have a loving family that features heavily in my life and has always supported me and encouraged me to be myself. They are the centre of my universe and the reason for my being. My parents divorced when I was younger but now have a great relationship – and as a bonus, I gained an extended family!

My mum is my heroine and the most caring person you could ever meet. She has had more than her share of life's struggles but doesn't let anything stand in her way when she puts her mind to it. She is the strongest person I know. But it was only later in life that I began to realise that 'strength' is often something people project so that they do not appear outwardly vulnerable. I have learnt that the root of my mum's strength stems from family and her desire to care, provide, and make sacrifices for them. I am so proud of my mum and hope people can see, at least, some of those values instilled in me.

I was so pleased when my mum met my now stepfather, who is one of the kindest men I have ever met. He has been in my life for over 20 years and is always happy to help (and I've called on him a lot!).

I'm sure he must have eased the burden on my dad quite significantly – I imagine I was very demanding as a teenage girl!

My dad has always been, and will always be, the main man in my life. As a child, no matter what I did, I would always have my dad wrapped around my little finger. Whether I was arguing with my brother, throwing the occasional 'sicky' or being told off for something I had done, he would always stick up for me and believe my version of events one hundred per cent of the time. (I think that still applies – even though I am now a grown woman in her early forties!)

Although he moved out of the family home as I approached my teenage years, I saw him often and he has always been supportive of everything I've done (and has also proven to be a very good sounding board). He also gave me the gift of my younger brother, of whom I am so proud. My dad is finally complete since rekindling his romance with a previous partner, who is now my stepmother. It makes me so happy to see my parents have ended up with the wonderful people they deserve. They may not have been the right fit for each other, but they are a perfect fit as close friends.

Growing up, my older brother and I had somewhat of a tumultuous relationship – as is common for siblings – but thankfully, we grew out of that and formed a closer connection with each other. When I was around 14, my brother moved abroad for a few months, which made me realise how much I missed him when he wasn't there. Before going, he had adorned my bedroom walls with hundreds of sticky notes with funny comments on (a lot of them making fun of my boyband posters – highly offensive at the time), which had meant the world to me, as I didn't think he liked me very much until that point! There was a quiet turning point in my life when my brother, once simply my companion in childhood mischief, became my steadfast protector, his presence a shield I hadn't known I needed. Being the only children in the immediate family meant we always had the limelight. I was more extroverted than my brother, but that position switched as we grew up.

Chapter 2

My Wider Family

My grandparents are possibly the most inspiring people you could ever meet.

My dad's parents were like second parents to me. They lived in the next street, and I was constantly round their house as a child, never giving them a moment's peace. My grandad and I often disagreed, mainly because we had differing opinions (for example, every time a motorist did something wrong, he would utter 'bet that's a woman driver' and I would immediately react and take offence), but we were extremely close, and I greatly admired his optimism in life and his love for my nan. I'll always remember his many words of wisdom and the life lessons he passed on to me in later years – 'always compromise' and 'never go to bed on an argument.' His passing was an extremely difficult and emotional time, which changed the lives of everyone that knew him.

My nan is my best friend. She is possibly my greatest supporter and confidante and has never failed to cheer me up. We have spent many hours chatting and putting the world to rights over the years, and it always amazes me how much compassion she has for everyone and anyone – she has the biggest heart and would do anything for my brothers and me. She is one of the kindest people I have ever met, and our bond will never be broken.

My mum's mum came from London originally and was evacuated to Wales as a 13-year-old child during World War 2. The suffering she had to endure in those early years is unimaginable. With two houses blown up and barely any belongings, my nan arrived in Wales with her younger siblings accompanying her. Those experiences shaped my nan's outlook on life and, rather than dwell on them, she grew to become successful and, together with my grandad, owned a successful grocery store for 40 years. She had a 'naughty' sense of humour and a wicked laugh that would echo around the room, and you couldn't help but join in. She grew up in the time of the Queen – there was only a year between them – and she would often say how good the Queen looked for her age, and compare their outlooks on life. Tragically, in 2022, both queens passed away within a few months of each other. Even their passings were similar: peaceful and at home.

My mum's dad was a kind, caring, intelligent man and very classy when it came to his attire. He was the definition of a classic gentleman. I remember him repeatedly saying to me, 'Maths and music go together in life.' But I think it was because I was good at both, and he wanted to encourage me. He'd greet us every Sunday afternoon, without fail, with a cheerful welcome and some freshly made crumpets with lashings of butter. Sadly, my grandad passed away in 2011, but he will always be remembered fondly by everyone who was fortunate enough to meet him – including the many customers that frequented his shop for 40 years!

My dad's brother was a generous uncle, and I was close to him as a child. I would often stay at his house and watch scary films, whilst we worked our way through a Chinese takeaway menu. He had a cross-collie dog named Sooty, with whom I would try to spend every possible minute. I referred to him as my 'cousin.' Sooty was found tied to a lamppost by my auntie (my mum's sister), who reported him to the police and then took him home to look after him until the owners came forward. No one ever did. After living abroad for many years, my uncle's return brought our family closer together, allowing us to cherish precious moments with him during his final years.

My auntie was fantastic! She was unable to have children of her own and so doted on my brother and me and, later on, my nieces. She had many health struggles, with multiple sclerosis (MS) ruling her daily activities, but you'd never guess the battle she was having inside, as she was always so cheerful. In fact, she was that much of a fighter, she gained her light aircraft pilot's licence, became Weight Watchers Woman of the Year, and, as she had had to leave her job in the police, she also participated in adult education classes and volunteered her time to help in a nursery. She was always smiling and thinking of ways to amuse everyone. My brother and I used to go round her house on a Sunday evening for cheese and crackers and to watch the WWF (wrestling). My auntie and I grew closer as I became older, so when the dreaded cancer reached out and pulled her from our lives, she left the darkest hole imaginable. Even my niece, who was only two at the time, still refers to her fondly.

My dad's brother and mum's sister had met through my parents a few years before and were married for several years before deciding to split. I imagine their divorce was a difficult time for everyone, but as my brother and I were so young, it didn't really affect us – especially as each remained our auntie and uncle.

I had an extremely loving childhood and was always smiling and laughing, so I am a perfect example of how mental health issues can creep up and affect you without warning. They just need a trigger to allow them to show themselves!

Chapter 3

Happy Memories

As a young girl, I was happy, lively, and full of confidence and optimism – certainly not words I would use to describe myself years later.

My first memory is holding hands with my mum on the way to pick my brother up from school. It was a long walk, especially when the rain came lashing down, but I enjoyed the smell of fresh air and the freedom of being outdoors. I looked forward to my brother finishing school, but found it very frustrating when he would go out to play with his friends and leave me indoors. But with a four-and-a-half-year age gap between us, I guess it was to be expected.

We lived in an old police house when my dad first became a policeman, and it was huge! In our hallway we had a lockable door leading into an office with a lockable door on the opposite side, which led into the adjoining police house. One evening, my brother and I couldn't find my mum and so ran through the office and into our neighbour's house, panicking. It turned out that our mum was only in the shower. (Luckily, we got on well with the neighbours, so they didn't mind too much.)

My dad was relatively new to the police force and was working all kinds of shifts, and, with my mum working part time, my dad's parents would often come round to look after us until my mum came home. One day I lost my nan! I anxiously searched each room in the house, even checking the cupboards, but I couldn't find her! My mum arrived home minutes later, and I told her that Nan had left us on our own. My poor nan was mortified (as she was only in the garden), and it's something we still laugh about to this day.

I attended the local nursery school and can remember my dad, in his new position as the community police officer, coming to give us a talk on safety. I was so chuffed that everyone knew he was my dad, and it instantly boosted my popularity, as suddenly my friends assumed that I was 'posh'.

Where I lived was a short walk away from the homes of my school friends, but it wasn't near enough for me to go out alone, as we were near a busy road with only a small bank and a shop nearby. Luckily, we had a huge front, side, and back garden, so there was plenty of room for playing outside.

When I was around four years old we moved to a different area, which had the bonus of being across the road from my grandparents, which I was overjoyed with. There was quite a large tump in the middle of our cul-de-sac, which was an awesome playing area and I made good use of it on sunny days. It was a more sociable area than I was used to and a more convenient location, especially as my dad's parents could now spend even more time with us without having to drive to see us. My school friends lived locally, and I also had other friends living nearby, who went to different schools.

Behind my grandparents' back garden there was a huge field, that was used by my primary school for sporting events, but you had to cross a small brook to get to it – unless you wanted to walk the long way round. It was there that I came across a girl who was lying on her back in the brook, shouting for her brother to help her. I found the situation hysterical, and couldn't stop laughing, but we soon became friends.

This field became the stage for some of my favourite adventures. My friends and I made swings from rope and branches, dens among the bamboo shoots, climbed trees and tried to make treehouses ('tried' being the operative word). We would push large stones into the brook to create paths to enable us to cross over to the field – which didn't always work. I remember one day convincing my dad (who was poorly at the time) to take me over the field to play football and to use a 'path' we had made to get there. One of the large stones moved and his foot slipped into the brook and the branch he was holding onto scraped across his collarbone and drew blood. I had never felt so guilty in my life!

It was around this time in my life that my nan became my best friend, as well as my neighbour. I would visit my grandparents daily and would always be welcomed with open arms and a tasty snack. My nan would often walk me to and from school and then cook my brother and me our tea – which was always served promptly at quarter past five, as per my mum's instructions. The menu was prepared by my mum, so there was no room for swaying away from the meal she wanted us to have.

My grandparents' house was padded from top to bottom whenever my brother and I visited. My nan was so worried about us hurting ourselves that every unit with a corner had a towel covering it; everything was washed thoroughly about twenty times; and anything that looked like it had the potential for a germ to rest on it was immediately removed from the room! I made up a 'washing hands' song that I would sing to my nan every time she walked me to school, as she was so obsessed with cleanliness. In hindsight, I think walking there and back was a chore for my nan, as I'd be touching walls, flowers and anything else that was in our path. She couldn't wait to get home so she could wash my hands thoroughly.

We would go strawberry picking in the summer months, on annual pantomime trips around Christmas, make pancakes on Pancake Day and have Halloween parties at their house, involving ducking apples, which my brother and I loved.

My grandparents always encouraged and supported me in whatever hobby took my fancy, and my nan would always keep my secrets so I wouldn't get a telling-off from my parents. I fell into the brook behind their house multiple times and would go back to theirs covered in mud, and my nan would clean me up the best she could, sometimes putting my trainers in the washing machine before I went home.

I loved staying at home with my nan in the week when everyone else was out, so I would time it right to feign a bad belly, as I knew she would worry and keep me off school. I got to watch things like *Supermarket*

Sweep and *Kilroy* in the mornings and *Murder She Wrote* in the afternoons. Lunch would consist of a HUGE ham salad sandwich – which was my favourite, as my nan used real butter and thick-cut bread. (It's funny how much nicer food is when it's made by someone else.) I loved those days, and, oddly, I always seemed to make a miraculous recovery by the time my mum came home from work!

Some of the best memories I have as a child were on the weekends, as my brother and I would sleep over at our grandparents' house, and we were each allowed to choose a video cassette film to rent from the local shop. We were so predictable; every time, without fail, I would select *Turner & Hooch* and my brother would choose *The Garbage Pail Kids Movie*. I would put my film on first, as I went to bed earlier than my brother, and his would follow later. My nan enjoyed watching my film – well, I assumed she did anyway – but she wasn't so fond of my brother's choice. (I think the title goes some way in explaining the context.) Those were the best nights – staying up later than we were meant to, eating chocolate, and watching a movie. The perfect weekend!

Chapter 4

Daily Life

I found weekdays very repetitive, but came to realise that I needed routine and structure in my life to create a purpose and to keep my mind occupied.

After school, I would play for an hour or two before having tea, and, during the winter months, when it was too dark to go outside and play, I would play on my games console in my bedroom or harass my brother to be allowed into his room to watch him play on his. Failing that, it would be an evening of TV downstairs with my parents, which usually consisted of either *The Bill*, *Dad's Army*, *The Brittass Empire*, or whatever delight was showing on one of the four channels we had.

I dreaded bedtimes, mainly because I hated having to turn off whatever I was watching, but also because I have always struggled with sleep and being able to shut my mind off for the night. However, I could see into the lounge of the bungalow behind my house from my bedroom window and, if I was lucky enough, the neighbours would be watching the same channel as my parents, so I could watch TV and hear the accompanying audio from downstairs. But most nights I would lie in bed reading a book by torchlight.

Every Saturday after lunch, my brother and I would have to walk to our local town with my mum and my nan so they could do a bit of shopping and have a natter. Our first port of call was always a café, where my nan would always buy us something chocolatey and a fruity item (usually Maltesers and fruit pastilles for me). Then we would have to endure an hour or two of walking around the most boring shops possible and wait while they discussed tea towels for what seemed like an eternity. The only consolation was that we were allowed to buy something from the toy stall in the indoor market to keep us happy (and well-behaved, too, no doubt).

After a couple of hours, we would return to my grandparents' house for tea, and my brother and I would play one of our favourite games, 'Let's see if we can pull grandad out of his chair'. Bless him, he would be sitting there watching the football results, and suddenly we would appear, take an arm each, and try to pull him up from the settee. I think he used to enjoy it as much as we did and would sometimes pretend to give in… until the last minute when he'd fall back into the settee with a groan (and a laugh).

On a Sunday, my brother and I would go to Sunday School with his friend and mum, who was a member of the congregation. The classes were split into age groups after the church service, and I had lots of fun. I once asked my mum why we were made to go to church, as she didn't go, and she said it was because she loved coming to the Christmas concerts they used to put on, and it also kept us from getting under her feet while she made dinner! One day, I suddenly lost interest in going, and everything became boring – a theme that seemed to follow me throughout my life!

After dinner on a Sunday, I would go across the road to visit my grandparents and my uncle, who would be there with his dog (and to get a share of their dessert). I would spend a couple of hours with Sooty each week and loved taking him on walks, playing and cuddling up to him. He would go crazy when he saw me and was one of the top runners in my 'best friend' category! He was very strong and always pulled on the lead. I remember tumbling into the road and grazing my arm one day, but instead of running away, he came and sat next to me, trying to lick my tears away. He would always protect me and growl at other dogs if they came near.

One day, Sooty escaped from my grandparents' house, and when my nan chased him across the road and tried to pull him back by his collar, he turned and bit her hand quite badly. My nan had to go to hospital, and I was told not to see Sooty again. I was devastated. From then on, I sneaked out every Sunday to climb over my nan's back garden wall to see him. He didn't make a noise; it's as though he knew the visits were secret! Eventually though, I was spotted. But I wasn't scolded by my grandparents, as the one thing my nan has always maintained is that Sooty was on his way to my house, and she believes he reacted in fear.

It sounds daft being so close to a dog that wasn't mine, but I loved him to pieces. I became a dog walker for some of my neighbours on the estate – back then, people were happy for you to 'borrow' their dogs. Even now, I can remember where each dog lived, its name and breed, yet I couldn't tell you anything about the owners!

Each Sunday afternoon, we would go to visit my mum's parents. When I was very young, they lived in the shop they ran in their local village, which was a great backdrop for our games! My brother would pretend to be the owner of the shop and donned various outfits with fake teeth/wigs/noses etc., and called himself 'Mr Weirdo'. My nan became 'Mrs Brown' and I was her daughter, who visited the shop where Mr Weirdo would try to sell us everything. (Thinking about it, I wonder if this influenced my brother's later career choice as a car salesman?!) The shop also had a large, dark, and very scary basement. It was originally used to store the stock for their shop, but, to us, it was the location of the exciting game 'Who can walk all the way down the stairs without turning the light on?'

My grandad would run around preparing snacks for us, and my nan would devise some games to keep us occupied. We played roulette, card games, ring toss – anything really! She would tell us a scary story about Worzel Gummidge and Sally on the ghost train at the fair, which would be sweetened by the arrival of, seemingly, hundreds of cakes/chocolates. We would leave their house worn out and our bellies full to the brim!

Chapter 5

Fun Times & Hobbies

My auntie briefly moved to a small village near my grandparents, in what is known as a one-up-one-down house. From the outside, it looked like a small extended bungalow, but inside it was my dream home. It had a tiny kitchen and bathroom, but a huge, open-plan living room, with her bedroom overlooking it, from a mezzanine level. There were skylights in the roof of her bedroom, which I thought was the best thing ever – my goal was to own a house just like this when I grew up. Looking back, I realise it would be completely impractical to live there comfortably, but at the time I thought it was amazing!

I stayed over the night before my auntie's wedding and was a bridesmaid on her big day (although I barely got any sleep due to her annoyingly nocturnal hamsters, Hammy and Sammy). The rain poured that day, but it failed to dampen the wedding spirit, and I was so chuffed to be a passenger in the wedding car and to visit a castle afterwards for photographs. I felt like a real-life princess and loved the attention that came with it, and, to make it even better, at the reception I got to dance with my new uncle's brother – who I had a crush on.

As I was growing up, I developed various musical hobbies, including playing the piano, the recorder, trombone and drums. Our next-door neighbour was a piano teacher, so I guess it was inevitable that I started learning the piano when I was young. My grandparents were so pleased that I had started having piano lessons, they bought me an organ for my bedroom. I played for a couple of years and passed a couple of gradings, but then I got bored and gave it up – unsurprisingly for me. I felt awful for my nan, who had been so excited that I was learning to play, especially as she'd taken the trouble to get an organ for me and have it delivered (and also for my parents, who now had this huge instrument in the house that nobody played!).

The recorder I played in school was a treble (slightly larger in size than the more common descant recorder, and with a lower pitch), but after a year or so, I also bored of that and gave it up. An instrument I played for quite a few years was the trombone. I used to go on residential camps with other schools and played as part of the orchestra in concerts. Unsurprisingly, I also gave up on that – although, in my defence, I had further to walk to comprehensive school, and the trombone isn't the lightest brass instrument to carry! I developed an interest in playing the drums, so my mum bought me an acoustic set for my bedroom. I wanted to have the garage soundproofed and get a full-sized drum kit, but my brother got to it first, and the garage became his gym area. Good job as, once again, I soon got bored. With the amount spent on having these larger instruments, the cost of lessons and the space they took up in the house, I'm sure my mum secretly wished I would settle for playing the triangle! I also took up horse riding lessons, but not long after, there was an incident involving me, the horse, the arena's open door and an impromptu gallop, so I gave that up too.

My favourite pastime, which I never got bored of, was reading. If I wasn't playing outside, then I was inside with my head in a book. My favourite author was Enid Blyton. Her books gave me a feeling of escapism, and her style of writing, with her colourful descriptions, made me feel like I was an actual part of the stories. I progressed onto other authors and enjoyed most genres – crime and thrillers being my preference as I grew up. I truly believe that reading is key in helping you step out of the real world for a time, and diving into your imagination. It can also be your saviour.

Chapter 6

Family Holidays

Each year, my parents would take my brother and me on holiday during the school's summer break. I loved these holidays, as it meant I got my parents' undivided attention, and we always had a whale of a time.

Our UK breaks were usually at a holiday park. I loved the clubhouses and the evening activities where I would take part in everything I could (much to my parents' dismay, as I regularly summoned them up to dance). I would always make friends with 'old people' – I think it must have been the fact that they were around my nan's age, and they gave me the most attention. My mum used to offer her apologies frequently, in case I was bothering them, but they seemed happy to chat to me. Surprisingly, one lady took my address and wrote to me a few times, becoming my pen pal! One of the best parts of a caravan holiday was the CD mix my brother would buy off the DJ at the end of the evening's show. He would use his holiday money, and I reaped the benefits by listening to it every time he put it on – a win-win situation for me; I didn't have to spend any money but still got to listen to the CD.

When I was four years old, my parents had saved enough to take us abroad to stay in a caravan in the south of France. I was so excited to go on an aeroplane, and I remember the holiday so well. It certainly wasn't what my parents had expected – but I enjoyed it!

When we arrived at the caravan, we found there was no linen for the beds, and we had to rent sleeping bags from the store down the road. I was excited to discover that my brother and I had bunk beds in our bedroom, and the first thing I did was to climb onto the top bunk to 'claim' my sleeping area. However, there was no guard on the top bunk, and, within seconds of climbing up, I fell off headfirst onto the floor. Understandably (but disappointingly), my parents decided my brother would be safer sleeping there.

There was no toilet in the caravan, but there was a communal toilet block in the middle of the caravan site. I decided a bucket wasn't sufficient in the middle of our first night, so I woke my dad to walk me to the toilet block. I quite liked this short walk – it was so peaceful and all you could hear was the sound of the crickets hopping around in the grass and the gentle breeze rushing through the trees around us.

There were swings near our caravan and my mum said I could go ahead and play on them. I went running off, with the hope of making some new friends. My mum came over after a few minutes to check on me, and, to her dismay, she found that I *had* made some new friends – three large Alsatian dogs. You could see the panic in her eyes as she saw me smoothing one of them while throwing a stick for the other two, and she called for me to come over to her immediately, then hastily walked me back to the caravan. When we got back, she scolded me for encouraging the dogs to follow us and explained they could have been aggressive or had fleas or any kind of disease. I was mortified that she could think like that and told her how lovely they were, and I was positive they didn't have fleas, but that didn't seem to pacify the situation. It's safe to say, I lost my new playmates as quickly as I had found them!

I remember the four of us casually walking to the beach one day, and my parents turning us around to walk to another beach while trying to disguise their laughter. I didn't understand why, but I later found out we had walked onto a neighbouring nudist beach and my brother had spotted some female naturists casually enjoying the sun.

One evening, we went to an event that was being hosted nearby, which included entertainment and a barbecue. It was awful! On arrival, we were told to turn our tops back to front to gain entry. My mum had a V-neck in the back of her top, so obviously declined. They put a lot of pressure on her to participate and she was really embarrassed saying no. The 'entertainment' was awful and consisted of local music and a couple of hook-a-duck stalls. The barbecue, which we were really looking forward to, was also disappointing. We were each allocated a manky burger and a sausage, which looked as if they were ready to walk to the bin themselves! We left shortly afterwards to visit a takeaway pizza café and took food back to the caravan to enjoy.

Even though the holiday did not go to plan, I must admit it was one of my favourites. We were all together and spent most of our time laughing at how weird it all was. After all, if it had been perfect, the chances are I wouldn't have remembered it!

Chapter 7

My Favourite Time Of Year

My favourite time of year was Christmas. Christmas to me meant family time, fun, chocolate and presents and has always been the most anticipated event of my year. My family members have always been equally excitable, and we would get together and make sure that everyone was involved and had a gift to open. It was, and still is, such a special time.

I would count down the days until Christmas and arm myself with the Argos catalogue to write down page numbers, item numbers and descriptions of everything I wanted. I would hand my wish list to my mum as though I was doing her a favour! My grandparents and uncle would visit us on Christmas Eve and walk my brother and me up to bed, singing 'Jingle Bells' while going up the stairs. We would make sure there was a mince pie and a glass of milk for Santa, and a carrot for Rudolph, before settling into bed. I would try to stay awake to catch Santa in the act of delivering presents, but I would inevitably fall asleep in the end. I used to wake around five thirty to go to my brother's room to ensure he was awake, before we woke my parents together. (We were less likely to be told off if we went together.)

In the run-up to Christmas, my auntie was just as excited as I was, if not more, and she would decorate her house from top to bottom with all the decorations you could think of. Everywhere you looked, there were flashing lights, tinsel garlands, moving Disney Christmas characters, snow globes, train tracks – the list was endless. To make your way to the kitchen, you would have to move out of the way of several dancing Santas and be careful not to knock over any of the Disney characters singing Christmas carols along the route. She would have all the Christmas films and started trimming up around the end of October!

My auntie loved having us over to make a fuss of and to play games with, and she would host various tea parties for the family to get together. She also loved Easter and Halloween and had decorations for these, too. She never changed, and with the arrival of my nieces, she remained exactly the same – they absolutely doted on her! She loved to write poems, get involved in arts and crafts and encourage any sort of creative behaviour – she was brilliant at decoupage, too. (Sadly, I did not follow in her creative footsteps.)

Christmas has always been a magical time for me, filled with joy and excitement. The twinkling lights, festive decorations, and the warmth of family gatherings create an atmosphere of pure happiness. I cherish the moments spent with loved ones, sharing laughter and creating memories that last a lifetime. The act of giving, whether it's a thoughtful gift or a simple gesture of kindness, brings me immense satisfaction and a sense of fulfilment. It's a time to reflect on the past year, appreciate the present, and look forward to the future with hope and optimism.

Chapter 8

School Days

Most of my friends were boys during my early school life, as I loved to play sports and I found them as active as me. Evenings and weekends were mainly spent playing football on the tump outside my home, climbing trees, jumping the brook, and playing games such as Mob or Fox & Hounds around my estate.

My best friend in infant school was amazingly bright. At six years old, when my mum asked him what he wanted to be when he grew up, he replied, 'An orthopaedic surgeon, or, if that fails, a *Playboy* photographer!' He lived right by my school and had a French au pair who was so much fun and let us get away with all kinds of things when the adults weren't around. I was devastated when his family moved hundreds of miles away, and we kept in touch for a few years via the telephone, letter and by sending Valentine's Day cards.

When I reached the top year of infant school, my mum told me I was being put in the same class as another girl who also had higher-than-average grades, as they wanted us to become friends. But, of course, when children are pushed together, they will immediately object – and that's where the bickering started. I have an old video cassette of our final Christmas concert at school, in which she was cast as The Grinch, and I was to sing a solo carol. I had wanted the leading part, so initially refused to be a soloist, but reluctantly agreed to do it if a few others joined me. I must say, though, we became good friends as we grew older and discovered we had similar interests – and we keep in touch to this day.

While in primary school, my best friend and I developed a crush on a new teacher. He was about 35 (which seemed ancient to us) and was always cracking jokes and making us laugh. We first met him when we were on a five-day trip called Camp Craft, which we attended with about twenty other school friends and another teacher. Initially, I didn't like him at all; in fact, he really upset me! There was a five-a-side football tournament being held one evening and the boys picked me for their team, but the teacher told me I couldn't take part, as I was female. I was devastated! When I complained that the rules didn't state that the teams couldn't be mixed gender, he relented, and I remember him apologising to me after the match – as I had scored the winning goal for our team!

I enjoyed playing football both inside and outside of school, and, as I was a good player and got on so well with boys, I was popular with my classmates and would always be picked first for teams. Also, I usually had one or two boyfriends at the same time – my 'inside school' boyfriend and my 'outside school' boyfriend. One boy in my class was a bit too keen on me and gave me various gifts, such as cassette albums, a Walkman, and a watch. My mum was very concerned about this and telephoned his mum. It turned out he had given me

Christmas presents that he'd received that year, so I was told to give them all back!

My favourite subject in school was, without a doubt, games. I was very sporty and loved taking part in any team sports or athletic competitions. On Sports Day, I came first in many of the races I took part in and was selected to compete in the District Sports Day. This was where schools in the district would come together to compete for the overall winning school title. I was entered into this event each year, and I loved it as it was a fun day with lots of spectators. In the last year of primary school, I became the female school captain of both the swimming and the athletics team, and I took the role very seriously. My dad used to take me training over the field behind my grandparents' house, and, as a result, I came first in the individual races and as a member of the relay team. The proudest day of my life up to that point was my school winning the overall event. As captain, I got to carry the (very large) plaque back to school and present it in Assembly the next day.

In my last year of primary school, I had a fantastic gymnastics teacher, who was very sporty. She gave me great advice on the transition to comprehensive school and encouraged my love of sports. She was a firm but fair teacher, whom I respected greatly. She tragically died of a brain tumour years later, and some old classmates and I attended the funeral to pay our respects.

It was during this last year of primary school that I first tried smoking. I went on a trip to a local park with some friends. After a while, the parents accompanying us settled down on their picnic blankets and a couple of the older boys moved away to a wooded part of the park. I followed them and had a puff of a cigarette offered to me. I remember everything started to spin and I felt so sick and had the biggest headrush ever! That was an incident that I wish had never happened.

I wish I could turn the clock back to re-live these years and to give me a chance to change some of the things that happened later. But I am grateful that I have these wonderful memories to treasure and that I had all the love I craved (and more) growing up. I never imagined the changes I was going to experience or believed that I would suddenly lose myself within the darkness of my own mind. The days of being carefree, confident, and happy were about to disappear.

Chapter 9

Transitioning To Comprehensive School

I was extremely optimistic about going to comprehensive school. I felt so grown-up and believed I was going to succeed in everything I did. I knew that this was a significant step in my life, and I was determined to make the most of it.

I was slightly nervous on that first morning while putting on my new school uniform (I didn't have to wear a uniform previously, and I wasn't used to the formalities), but a few of my old classmates had arranged to meet so that we could walk up together, so my nervousness soon turned into excitement. My new school was a 25-minute (mainly uphill) walk through town, and we would stop at the local shops on the way to get our stash of chocolate. These shops opened earlier than others, as they no doubt benefitted from the vast number of school children eager to spend their lunch money on goodies before school.

Before leaving primary school, I was asked to submit a list of people in my friendship group, and give it to my teacher so that they could try and keep as many of us together as possible. This system clearly didn't work! After narrowing my friendship group down to only six names, I entered my new class with only one friend and twenty-nine other children from three different schools! I was so upset. I asked my previous teacher why this had happened, and she explained it was because my friend and I were considered independent and could happily make new friends from different schools (a compliment of sorts?!). My new form had a mix of characters, whom I initially found intimidating, so I would meet up with my friends in other classes at breaktimes to catch up on any gossip and ensure I remained a part of the group.

The first year of comprehensive school was an eye-opener and probably shaped my behaviour for the rest of my school journey. I always raised my hand to answer questions posed by the teacher, and I was quick to volunteer for anything requested of the class. I soon realised this was not the way forward, and I was going to be classed as a swot, which was not what I wanted to be known as. So, I quickly changed my behaviour.

It was at the end of the first term that I fell out with my friend who had accompanied me from primary school. This was at such an awkward time, as we were at her birthday party when we fell out, and I didn't really know anyone else who would be on my side. I spent the evening alone, playing skittles in a different room from where the disco was being held, when another girl from my form class came and joined me. That was when I made one of my best friends, who was with me throughout school. She seemed to know almost everyone, and I soon became friends with them, too.

In the first year, form classes were not separated by the perceived ability levels of pupils but were taught as a whole. My class became the most notorious of our year group, and we would have regular tellings-off by department heads, and they would sometimes attend our classes to supervise our behaviour with supply teachers. I realised that the way forward was to make people laugh, so I often joined in with the class antics. But I sometimes pushed the boundaries a bit too far and would get sent to stand outside the classroom door in the corridor. It was at this point that I realised that piano and trombone playing were not thought of as cool, so I gave them both up and decided to stick with athletics.

I wanted to join a girls' football team, so my dad did a bit of research and found a local team that trained on a Monday evening and played matches on a Sunday afternoon. I was nervous going to my first training session, but everyone was welcoming, and the coach was a nice guy who constantly told (poor) jokes! It was in football training that I met a good friend who happened to be the same age as me and was from the same area as most of my classmates.

For the first couple of years my dad would take me to training on a Monday evening, picking up my friend on the way, and come to every match we played – whether we played at home or away. Following my parents splitting up and my younger brother being born, my dad wasn't as readily available, so the coach would often give us a lift to the away matches, and we had the best laughs on the way. I enjoyed playing for the team for around 4–5 years, but as I got older, there was a change in management and some unrest in the team, so I decided to leave.

My first school year flew by, and I made some great friends and spent a lot of time with them outside of school. I was excelling in athletics, had joined the netball team, picked up a trophy on prize evening for being the 'best female sportsperson' in my year group, and also equalled a javelin school record.

It was towards the end of this school year that I started feeling a little unconfident and unsure of myself. I put this nagging doubt in my head down to the fact that I was in a new school with new friends, and I was still trying to find my feet. I felt stupid for even having negative thoughts, as there were so many people in the world who were worse off than me, so why was I feeling sorry for myself? How I wish I had spoken to someone at the time… I might have avoided all the upset that followed. But back then, I kept telling myself that I was happy and everything was great.

Chapter 10

Becoming A Teenager

By the second year of comprehensive school, I had changed into someone who enjoyed making my classmates laugh, and I became a bit of a force to reckon with. I thought that to be popular, I needed to create an image that meant no one would want to cause me any trouble, but, equally, they would still want to be friends. I believe it's a common misconception among 'almost-teenagers' that you need to appear confident and in control in school or you risk being ignored – or even worse, bullied!

It was around this time that things didn't seem quite right at home between my parents. I had never really known them to show affection towards each other publicly, and one day, my dad called me into my bedroom and sat on my bed for a chat. He told me he was going to be moving out of the family home but would be living nearby. My first reaction was to ask if I could go with him, but he said I wouldn't be able to. Then, after I'd thought for a few minutes, I agreed it was probably a good idea for them to split up if they were unhappy.

The next morning, before school, I went over to my grandparents' house to tell my nan about my conversation with my dad. She was understandably worried about the situation but tried to reassure me that everything would be fine. It was one of the biggest mistakes I ever made. By not giving my parents the opportunity to explain it to her themselves, it caused a lot of worry, and I'm guessing I didn't present it in the way that they would have. My grandparents were terrified that we would move away and that they wouldn't see my brother and me nearly as often – my mum was like a second daughter to them – and they were so scared their relationship would be lost.

My dad moved out a short time later into a rented house that was close to a school friend of mine, and I would stay there from time to time. By now, my brother was 'too old' to want sleepovers, so he didn't come with me to our dad's house. I would alternate where I woke up on my birthday and on Christmas mornings, and where I would go for Christmas dinner. And I used to stay at my dad's fairly often, – at weekends and sometimes during the week – because it was in a far more convenient location for walking to school. At home, I acted like all was okay and that I was content with the situation. I never felt comfortable talking about my feelings and preferred to lock things away, doing my best to ignore them. My teenage years certainly showed me this was a mistake!

I then got into a bit of trouble in school and would drive my teachers mad. I was in the top stream for every subject, but I would always get told off for something or other and would be moved to sit by myself at the front of the class. On occasion, I would be told to stand outside the door for the rest of the lesson and then I'd have to endure a telling-off from our head of year. I hated it when this happened, as they would always follow it with a phone call to my mum. I dreaded those calls! I would be sitting anxiously at home, listening for the sound of my mother's heels walking down the driveway after work, for her to come in and say, 'Can we speak in the conservatory please?' I knew this meant I was in trouble. Possibly the most embarrassing moment was being told to leave a lesson and sit in with the head of English and her class for the rest of the period. I thought this was funny, until I walked in and realised she was teaching my brother's A-level class! I'm not sure who was more embarrassed, him or me.

I got bored in most lessons and would look for distractions, which unfortunately meant I must have annoyed a lot of people who wanted to learn. Luckily for me, I had a partner in crime, and together we were often getting told off for chatting or answering back. We used to get separated on school trips – but always found ways to be reunited – which would result in us getting into trouble for the umpteenth time that week. The only lesson where I didn't get bored was games. I still loved sports and had a competitive nature when it came to team games or individual events. I won the Victrix Ludorum trophy for three consecutive years, for outstanding sporting achievement. But by the time I was in my mid-teens, I had lost interest in sports and preferred to simply hang out with friends.

My brother and I were typical teenage siblings; we usually annoyed each other. One evening when we were rowing, I threw my cup at him, which caught him on the bridge of his nose and drew blood. In retaliation, he ripped out the eyes of Flopsy, my cuddly soft rabbit. I was distraught! I loved my cuddly toys, and this was too much for me, so I marched down to the local supermarket, where I knew my mum was shopping, and told her what had happened (obviously leaving out the part where I had thrown my cup), and helped her finish the food shop. When we got back, suffice to say, my brother told my mum the full story and I didn't get any sympathy. The next day in school, a teacher came up to me to ask why I'd thrown something at my brother – she'd seen the mark on his nose – and I was secretly gutted to be thought of as a ruffian.

During football games on the weekend, I would get angry at the opposition and wanted them to create a scene so I couldn't be blamed for my reactions. It was much the same in school. I was quite popular with both boys and girls, so I never really had any bother, and people seemed to listen to me and respect my views. I had a great range of friends in school, all with different backgrounds and upbringings, and I was lucky enough to be invited into many of their lives in one way or another – whether it was to stay the night, go to their houses for tea or be invited to family events/holidays. I always went with a smile on my face and would adapt my demeanour to suit the company I was in. I have never bullied anyone and would happily call someone up on it if I witnessed it. I was a real softie and would easily get upset if I thought I had offended someone. Of course, no one knew that, though – except my mum!

What my friends' parents wouldn't have guessed was that I had a flourishing business in school selling cigarettes to my classmates. I would pay £2.20 for a packet of 20 cigarettes, and then sell them for 50p each, or two for 80p. It was great – I would earn enough to buy a packet each day, have a Chinese takeaway deal for my lunch and still have money left over for chocolate and sweets. My friends still chuckle about this and tell me how I ripped them off.

Around this time, my nan became poorly and wasn't up to having visitors. The stress of my parents splitting up, along with the potential impacts this could have had on the relationships that she had with my mum, my brother and me, was just too much for her to bear. I used to spend my pocket money and any leftover dinner money buying flowers for her, and I would go round to her house each evening to sit with her and chat away about my (usually uninteresting) day. She has always said how persistent I was, especially for a thirteen/fourteen-year-old, and how much these visits used to lift her spirits.

I felt a lot of sadness at the time of my parents' separation, but I put those feelings on the back burner, as, in the grand scheme of things, they seemed childish and attention-seeking. However, I desperately wish I'd spoken to my mum at this point, as I know full well she would have listened to me and helped in any way she could have. I knew that my brother and I were always the main priority, but I felt like I would be adding to the stress, so I chose to keep my feelings inside and appear to carry on as normal. I enjoyed maintaining the 'don't care' persona, as it meant no one would ask me about anything personal. With my friends, I would turn everything into a joke and was very blasé about most things.

The one positive I can confidently say about myself, is that I have always been thoughtful and empathetic towards others and would happily spend my time and money on making others happy. Some may refer to it as 'people-pleasing', but I call it being kind and understanding.

Chapter 11

Losing Control

As I progressed into my teenage years, I felt myself slipping into a deep, dark void. Outwardly, I appeared fine and seemed to cope very well with everything, but inside, I was in turmoil. I remember lying awake at night, unable to quiet my racing thoughts, feeling completely alone, despite being surrounded by family and friends. This is the unfathomable thing about mental health issues – they can creep up and engulf you without warning, and you can be unaware of what triggers them.

It started with taking tablets. I would creep downstairs, silently, at night, and search for the paracetamol – I didn't take enough to achieve (what I thought was) the desired effect, but enough to make me feel like I was accomplishing something. I remember taking some to school once, and knocking them back in the toilets while pretending I didn't know anyone could see me. Someone obviously intervened and stopped me and made me flush the rest down the toilet. I don't know why I did this, but it must have been a cry for attention, as I had done it in full view of someone, feeling safe in the knowledge that I would be stopped. I made them promise not to tell a teacher, as I didn't want anyone thinking that I was unstable, and more importantly, I didn't want my family to know.

After this episode, I didn't take tablets anymore unless they were prescribed, and even now I hate taking medication, as, subconsciously, it reminds me of this dark time. Instead, I started to self-harm. This way, I could pretend visible marks were from usual day-to-day activities and suspicions wouldn't be aroused.

They started as minor scratches on my forearms, which were visible enough for people to ask about, but not prominent enough for them to think I was responsible. This suited me for a while, as people would show concern but equally didn't explore the details. But then I would feel angry inside that no one seemed to realise I was unhappy and needed help. This wasn't anybody's fault, as I kept it all hidden, and my family didn't see anything – after all, I was still full of jokes and sarcasm.

I was in a Catch-22 situation, as, on the one hand, I wanted people to probe so that they would know that I was struggling, but on the other hand, I didn't want my family to know, and so I hid all visible signs. Over time, I became angry with myself for feeling this way and I truly believed that I didn't add anything special to anyone's life. I felt like I was a burden and wanted to punish myself to release those thoughts for a time. I was in my own delusional bubble and was destined to race towards chaos.

I wanted to be out of this world and spent a lot of time looking for reasons to convince myself that I deserved to be here. The only reason I could come up with was my family. And as much as I wanted to escape my seemingly pointless existence, I couldn't bring myself to inflict that kind of pain on them. But this upset me even more, as I felt I would have to sacrifice my happiness in order to save my family from dealing with loss.

Looking back, I realise that those moments were a cry for help. I was struggling with feelings of isolation and inadequacy, and the act of taking tablets or harming myself were ways to express my inner turmoil. It was a misguided attempt to gain control over my emotions and to make others aware of my pain.

I had felt trapped in this endless black hole, where every day felt like Groundhog Day. I would put on my 'invisibility mask' every morning and take it back off when I was alone at home. I would sit in my bedroom, trying to think of different ways to hurt myself – while also thinking of excuses to explain the marks. I discovered that one way was to rub the underside of a shoe across my arm repeatedly. It looked like a carpet burn to the outside world, but it was a reminder to me of how worthless I felt. For a time, this seemed like a reasonable way to vent my frustration. Then I became way too brazen, and it all came crashing down around me.

Chapter 12

A Hard Lesson To Learn

One Sunday afternoon, I came home from a football match and ran straight upstairs to my bedroom and dragged a shoe across my forehead a few times. I went back downstairs and said to my mum that I had grazed my head playing football. No one had noticed the injury when I first got back, but I convinced everyone it had only just flared up, as I'd scratched it. The next day in school, I was called to the deputy head's office, where I was told a teacher had raised a concern about me, and she wasn't accepting my excuse for the injury. I got upset and she drove me to the local GP surgery, asked a nurse to tend to the wound, and left me there. She reminded me that my bag was in her office, so I'd have to return to school to collect it, as I wouldn't be able to sneak home without my house keys.

I was mortified! Not only was it extremely embarrassing, but the way in which it was handled was disgusting! I felt judged and stupid, and even more worryingly, I was left alone while feeling like this! A child of 15! These were the main reasons that I didn't tell anyone about my inner struggles in the first place! I panicked that my friends would find out what had happened and think I was 'mad', and about how I was going to deny this to my mum when the school inevitably called her.

I reluctantly walked back up to school a little while later, scared of what people would think about the dramatic bandage wrapped around my head, and I went to the deputy head's office to report back. She told me she'd called my mum and I should return to class. Unbelievable! Thank goodness mental health issues are now more likely to be addressed and identified earlier on, and there are more readily available teachers who want to help with the wellbeing of students. I simply can't imagine where we would be now without people who take the time to understand and care about mental health in young people.

I remember walking into class, laughing at the bandage wrapped around my forehead, and taking it off to reveal a simple-looking graze. I told my friends that a teacher had overreacted, and I'd had to go to the doctor's for this measly cut, and we all laughed it off.

That evening, after hearing the familiar clicking of my mum's shoes walking down the drive, I waited in readiness with my excuses for this behaviour. But they didn't work. My mum was upset that I hadn't spoken to her about how I felt about things and said that an appointment had been made for us with an educational psychologist at school the next day. I was devastated! I wouldn't talk to family members, never mind being interrogated by a stranger who, I assumed, would be judging me.

The next day I told my friends that I had to see a psychologist in school because of my recent behaviour. They knew my behaviour wasn't an issue compared to some people, but nevertheless they accepted my admission and didn't press me any further – even though I'm sure they knew all wasn't right with me. My mum came to the school, and we were ushered into an office where the psychologist was waiting for me with her notepad.

I immediately knew that I wouldn't be speaking to her and wanted to leave. The way I felt I was looked at and judged was enough for me to put my barriers up and put on my 'mask'. Within the first couple of minutes, she declared I was clinically depressed, as I hadn't made great eye contact with her, and that was the underlying problem. Really?! She said I had a serotonin chemical imbalance, which had nothing to do with my feelings. Come on – even *I* knew that couldn't be it. I cried to my mum afterwards and begged her not to make another appointment, as I hated being judged by someone and I felt it would make me worse. She thought about it for a while and then agreed to hold off booking another appointment to see if I could come through this with the support of those who knew.

This experience taught me the importance of seeking help and talking about my feelings rather than resorting to self-destructive behaviours, and since that day I have never harmed myself again. I'm not sure if it was a combination of being embarrassed that people found out, the feeling I had of upsetting my mum or the realisation that it was not this type of attention I wanted. Even though I didn't hurt myself again, I was aware that the black shadow resting on my shoulder was there to stay… and might never leave.

I don't know if my mum ever told anyone about the visit to my school, but I do know that no one has ever mentioned it to me.

Chapter 13

Maintaining Balance

Following this incident, I plodded on as normal – whatever I perceived 'normal' to be – and had some good times along the way. But the presence of darkness was always there, waiting to envelope me into its shadows again. For the most part, I maintained a balance between sadness and appearing to be high-spirited to others, but sometimes I would find myself feeling lost and having negative thoughts. I got through these instances by thinking about my family, and how I wouldn't want them feeling responsible for any thoughts I may have had. But I could never get rid of the nagging feeling of being an 'outsider' and not really fitting in anywhere.

Another phase I went through, a form of self-harm I guess, was by piercing my own ears. I had three holes in my ears already, but decided I wanted more; at one point I had nine earrings in one ear. Then I decided I wanted to be different and to really stand out, so I decided to pierce my hand. I pierced the skin in between my thumb and forefinger – but there was nothing to hold the stud in place once it had healed. My friends thought it was hilarious and very bizarre – we still laugh about it now when they remind me about it.

Another time, I decided I wanted a lip ring, so I pierced my lip using a hoop earring and went straight round to my friend's house after it was done, as my lip had swollen and I didn't want my mum to see it. My friend thought I was mad and encouraged me to take it out, but I liked it. I would take it out at home and put it back in for school, keeping my hand over my mouth so that teachers wouldn't see it. Unfortunately, I only got away with it for one and a half days before someone noticed and sent me to the head of my school year. I told him I would take it out and pleaded with him not to tell my parents, and he believed me and agreed not to tell anyone. After that, I took it out and never did anything like it again.

It's as though I needed people to trust in me; I would respect that and not repeat the behaviour. I don't know why I needed this certainty from others, as my family members have only ever shown trust in me, but that is all I can surmise when looking back.

When my brother moved abroad for a few months, the house felt empty. I'd been used to having a house full of visitors, and we would host barbecues or Christmas parties etc. Suddenly, it was quiet. I missed my brother terribly, as did my mum, but this time together definitely brought my mum and me closer.

Saturday evenings were my favourite time of the week. We would order a Chinese takeaway, then my mum would pull up her chair next to mine, in front of the TV, and we would have the chocolate of my choosing and watch a film picked from my brother's vast array of videos. I never went out on a Saturday evening to the local park with all my friends (which was previously unheard of), as I enjoyed staying in with my mum so much. I think this addressed my feelings of 'not making much of a difference to anyone's life', as it was obvious to me how much my mum also enjoyed these evenings.

I would telephone my brother while he was away, and he would fill me in on his life abroad – which made me very envious! One evening, he passed the phone to his new girlfriend, whose Essex accent I struggled to understand, and it's safe to say we had the most bizarre conversation ever – neither of us really understanding what the other was talking about. When he returned a few months later with his girlfriend, they came to pick me up from school and she was wearing my shoes! I thought it was a bit odd. I'd forgotten she had come straight from the sunshine and would have no suitable shoes for the weather back in the UK. I still had difficulty in understanding her accent – which made for an awkward half an hour sitting in a car together while my brother 'popped' to his mate's house. I didn't think we would have much in common at all, but she turned out to be one of my best friends – and later became my sister-in-law.

I became very security-conscious and paranoid when I was at home alone. I had a fear of fire when I was younger, and my mum used to keep my bedroom door open at night with the landing light shining into my bedroom, as I had recurring nightmares about the house being on fire and my dad not escaping with us. These dreams seemed to fade over time, but they were replaced by ones of people breaking into our house at night. This fear intensified when my brother was away. I felt safer when my dad had lived with us, as he was a policeman, and when my brother took over the role of being 'the man of the house', I had also felt reassured. But when they were both gone, I felt a little more vulnerable.

A long time later, my mum introduced me to a man she had met at work. I took to him straight away and always wanted him to stay at our house. My mum didn't want me to feel rushed, and she was very cautious about my brother and me meeting somebody new, unless she was certain they were going to be entering our lives forever. Her sixth sense was correct – he became our stepdad! I used to harass my mum to let him stay over, as there were three benefits for me: first, I loved seeing my mum happy; second, I really liked him and felt safer with him there; third, a major bonus, he sometimes smoked. So… she would be less likely to smell cigarettes on me when I came home!

Eventually, she invited him to live with us, and we later moved to a newly built estate, which was closer to some of my school friends. Even there, I couldn't shake off the feeling of being watched or the feeling that someone was already in the house. I don't know why I had this feeling, as I loved the new house, and it was very secure. Looking back, I guess it might have been my anxieties showing up in a different form from how they had previously appeared.

The house had an alarm, but we didn't know the combination, so my dad got in touch with someone he knew who could come and reset it. That was great – until we had the garage converted and I spotted a potential way that someone could break into the house without triggering the alarm motion sensors. So my mum had an extra lock put onto the new door leading into the hallway, which rectified the situation. But I would still always have a friend sleeping over if I was alone overnight.

I remember my mum and stepdad staying in an airport hotel prior to going on holiday, and I called them up late at night, panicking, as I was convinced that I could smell smoke in the stairway. I was so upset that my stepdad said he would collect the car from the parking compound and make the long drive home just to reassure me. After speaking for a time on the telephone, my mum calmed me down and I realised there was no reason to be alarmed and there was no fire at home. Suffice to say, I roped a friend into staying over for the rest of the time that they were away.

My GCSE exams were on the horizon, and I had fallen behind in mathematics (mainly because I had been skiving), so my stepdad offered to tutor me in readiness. He was a civil engineer and found the syllabus easy to teach. I am proud to say I passed my maths exam with an A – which was completely unexpected – and achieved A and B grades in my other subjects. On results day, my maths teacher came up to me and apologised for suggesting that I sit a lower paper, as he had obviously got it wrong. I suddenly had the utmost respect for him, as most teachers claimed they were attempting reverse psychology by saying I would fail because I wasn't putting the effort in. Whatever.

I stayed on to do A levels and achieved the grades needed to get me onto my preferred law course at university. I remember seeing one of my teachers after collecting my results, and she said people like me annoyed her, as her daughter had received lower grades even though she'd always turned up to lessons and revised thoroughly. I felt a bit uncomfortable at first, but then I saw it as a hidden compliment.

I found that by keeping myself busy, I was able to balance my thoughts and shelve any worries or anxieties in the back of my mind. As a result, I was constantly doing something with friends, visiting my family or working.

Chapter 14

Life Beyond The Classroom

My first part-time job was working on the markets selling general knick-knack items. I worked on a local stall and would travel miles with the stallholders to various markets around the region. We also covered big events, and I really enjoyed the banter and meeting lots of new people. Following this, I got a job in a local garden centre, which was the best job in the world around Christmas time, as I controlled the Christmas music and manned Santa's grotto. This was the perfect job for me, and I loved entertaining the children queuing up to see Santa. Once Christmas was over, I tended to lose interest in the job, but as they started to create their huge Christmas land display, from around July, I threw myself into helping with that.

After working there for a while, I applied for a role in a banking group, which paid a lot more and had the added bonus of my friend also working there. This probably wasn't the best idea. We would usually stay at each other's houses on weekends and we enjoyed going out, so we had limited motivation, which would often mean calling in sick at the same time. After a few months, I got bored of that job and applied successfully for a waitressing role – but I quit before my first shift, as I didn't fancy travelling there in the snow. I also obtained a job at a pub, but when I found out my friends were attending a nearby festival that day, I got into my car and left before the end of my first shift. (I did post my work uniform back to them in the mail.) I was also successful in gaining a part-time job in a DIY store, but I called in sick on the first day and never went in.

After my A levels, I joined university to study Law and Criminology – but the boredom demon got hold of me once again, and within three months, I had quit university and was selling Christmas trees! I could tell my family were gutted, but they supported my decision. Once the Christmas period was over, I started working in a travel agency, but then left that to work for something more local. Unsurprisingly, I soon got bored! I looked for ways out and decided to apply to attend a university over a hundred miles away, to take a course that was due to start within the next few months. Because of my grades, I was accepted straight away, so I had to break the news to my parents. They were surprised, as they'd had no idea that was what I wanted to do, but they were happy for me. The only problem was, I had limited time to get everything prepared – from accommodation to student loans.

Despite the frequent changes in my situation and the uncertainty that came with them, I found solace in the support of my family. Their unwavering belief in my abilities gave me the confidence to keep pushing forward. These experiences, though seemingly disconnected, were all stepping stones that led me to where I am today. They shaped my character and prepared me for the challenges that lay ahead.

Chapter 15

Moving Away

My mum and stepdad drove me up to Birmingham to help me settle in. It was a bit disconcerting that the security staff, in the introductory chat, handed out personal alarms to everyone for protection! The room that was to be my home for the next year was small to say the least. To make it worse, I was housed in the first room you passed as you came up the stairs, so all I could hear was the constant banging of the stairwell door. I didn't have an ensuite, which devastated me, and the communal bathroom was gross. The communal kitchen, across the hallway from my room, smelt of damp, and I wasn't too happy with the security of the halls as a whole! I came up with a few possible ways in which someone could break in unnoticed if they really wanted to. The only consolation was that the girls in the neighbouring bedrooms seemed nice. When the time came for my mum to leave that afternoon, we were both really upset. It was my first time away from home; I'd never had to fend for myself before. It was a scary realisation!

On the first night, a group of us went to the on-site student union before heading into the city centre for drinks. It was a good night, and I was feeling a lot better about moving there – until it was time to return to my room! I spent all night watching the light under the crack of the door and listening to the unfamiliar sounds that surrounded me. I put a chair under the door handle so that it couldn't be pulled down and opened easily, and a little pile of bric-a-brac in the entrance, so that if I did fall asleep, I would be woken up by the noise of someone entering.

The second day saw the start of freshers' week, which was my introduction to university life. There were lots of stalls and information points and plenty of sales reps hoping to lure naïve students into signing up for things they didn't need. I became a sucker to one such rep who was offering a 'free' popcorn maker to everyone that took out a credit card with them that day. It seemed like such a bonus at the time, but it signalled the start of my spiralling debts. (And I never even used the popcorn maker!)

Later that day, I was confronted by a daddy-longlegs in my room, and I ran out terrified, slamming the door behind me. After a few minutes, I crept back in to spray some deodorant at it (it was all that I had to hand) and it pounced at me from behind the door. I turned on my heel and bolted to get out, breaking my middle toe in so doing. One of my neighbours came to see what the commotion was about and found me sitting in the stairwell, barely able to stand up. She helped me limp to an on-site nurse, who told me it was broken, but unfortunately, all they could do was strap it up. I was gutted! Not only was I in a strange place on my own, but I was also unable to go out and socialise with my newfound friends, as I could barely walk. However, on the plus side, one of the girls had managed to get rid of the intruder for me.

Those first few days seemed to drag on forever. I didn't feel safe at night, and I found myself welcoming the noise of the door banging at the top of the stairs in the early hours, as it signalled everyone returning from their nights out. I have always been very particular about cleanliness in bathroom areas, so I would wait for the bathroom to appear empty before going in to clean the area I needed to use. To my horror, the shower areas were not in locked cubicles, so I bought a tap mixer extension head to attach to one of the baths in a lockable cubicle to use. Anyone who has tried to navigate their way around one of these will know how useless they are; they slip off the taps and the temperature constantly fluctuates – no matter which way you turn the taps or how patient you are in trying to adjust them.

Every week, I would buy a return train ticket to come home for the weekend – which kind of defeated the object of moving away, but it made me happy knowing I was going back to a safe and clean environment, and I would look forward to nights out with my friends. My sister-in-law and I went out almost every Saturday to a popular entertainment venue that hosted cabaret shows, mainly featuring drag acts. They were hilarious and we knew we would be guaranteed a good night there. We also became friends with the staff, which meant the admission fee was always waived, and it became our regular haunt. I slowly began to realise that maybe university life wasn't for me after all.

My mum came to stay with me on one of the rare weekends I decided not to go home, and as soon as we got into the town centre, someone was mugged right in front of us! It took me hours to convince my mum that

I was safe and that witnessing a mugging wasn't an everyday occurrence. Other than that unfortunate episode, we had a nice weekend shopping and eating out. The sleeping arrangements were cramped, as my room was so small and there was only my single bed, so I slept on the floor between the bed and the desk in a sleeping bag. Although we didn't really have any room to move about, it was surprising how empty it felt when my mum left, and I was alone again.

I made friends with the girls in my halls, but I became a bit of a recluse once the novelty of going to new nightclubs had worn off. I tended to stay in my room a lot and would watch DVDs, listen to CDs and read books over and over, dwelling on everything and wondering how I had got myself into this situation. In keeping with my usual behaviour, I soon got bored with the course I was studying. I barely went to any lectures, as I had lost interest in the subject and motivation to attend. I felt embarrassed to admit that I wanted to leave after springing the initial move on everyone at such short notice and kept up the appearance of feeling perfectly content with my life. When I came home for the Christmas period, I decided to quit and only return to get my belongings. I'd lasted one term!

Chapter 16

Becoming A 'Real' Adult

After returning from university, I moved back in with my mum and needed to get a 'proper' job, so I went about applying. I had a job in a shop, in which I lasted a day before quitting, one in a health and safety company, but I didn't return after my lunch break, and a call centre job, in which I stayed for two days, before finally settling back into the travel agency that I had previously worked for. After a year or so, I decided to look for a salary increase without the need to work overtime, so I left to join an organisation that inspected healthcare settings. I stayed there for three years and really enjoyed my job. I had a great boss, who became a good friend, along with pretty much everyone else who worked there. We were a social bunch and would often arrange nights out and get together for lunch away from the office. At one point, it was almost every day!

I was around 20 when I moved out of my mum's, as a family member was moving abroad and asked if I would like to stay in their house until they sold it. I was excited and took them up on the offer straight away. But it suddenly hit me – I was a 'real' adult! I would have bills and would have to pay for my own food and toiletries. I realised that this would leave me with little disposable income, so I returned to the travel agency to work there part time, alongside my full-time job. I worked Monday to Friday in my full-time job and three evening shifts a week and every Saturday or Sunday in my part-time job. It was exhausting, but I still found time to go out every Friday and Saturday night, and any free evening I had during the week. I was definitely burning the candle at both ends and I began to wonder what the point was of living on my own if I never wanted to be in the house on my own.

I got my first dog, a border-collie cross, and named him Pepsi. I came across an advert selling border collies (I wanted a dog like my childhood bestie, Sooty) from a farm about an hour's drive away, so I called them and arranged to pick him up the following night. My friend came with me to pick him up, and after getting lost in mountainous lanes for over an hour, we found the farm. It was cold and dark by the time we got there, and we were greeted by torchlight and led to a large shed where the puppies were kept.

I was appalled when the lady opened the door to see that there was no bowl of water for the two remaining puppies she had in there, and they certainly weren't concerned about cleanliness. She offered us the remaining puppy for half price. I couldn't believe it! I wished I'd been able to take the other pup away from her, but I knew one would be enough of a struggle. My friend, who wasn't keen on dogs, even contemplated taking the other puppy out of the situation. The next day, I reported the farm to an animal charity, which later confirmed that the property was being used as a puppy farm and they would be closing it down. Thank goodness for that!

Bringing Pepsi home was the best feeling ever. I had always wanted a dog and couldn't wait to settle him in his new home. The first people he met were my grandparents, who fell in love with him straight away. He was tiny, black all over with a white chest, and very fluffy. As he grew, I found that he absolutely loved people and was the most energetic dog I had ever come across. So much so, that I had to take him to private lessons with a dog trainer to learn how to curb his excitement and to stop him jumping on everyone who entered the house. He did well at training, but after a few sessions, I decided to take the training forward myself.

He was a very intelligent breed and would do basic tricks easily, such as rolling over, bowing, sitting on his hind legs, and walking on his hind legs, but I still couldn't find anything to tire him out. I would walk or run with him as much as I could, and constantly played with him in the garden, but he was extremely boisterous and could keep going for hours. I had got myself into a very tricky situation, as I was working almost every day and, even though I would go home during my lunch breaks, I struggled to keep him occupied. I came home one day to find he had ripped the lino up from the kitchen floor, which I quickly replaced with carpet.

I then bought my rabbit, Diesel, who was apparently a dwarf rabbit – although he looked like he'd eaten the other six dwarves by the time he was a few months old! Bizarrely, for a dog and a rabbit, they got on amazingly well. I would leave them to run around together, and if Diesel got fed up and wanted to sit in the sun quietly, he would sit there and not move until Pepsi gave up trying to play with him. I was lucky to have two animals with such good temperaments.

I liked this house and had been used to staying in it as a child, but I still couldn't get rid of the feelings of anxiety and paranoia. On a few occasions, I left the house late in the evening and went to my mum's to stay the night. These feelings lessened a bit once I had Pepsi for company, but then my fear was that someone would break in and hurt him, too. It was relentless and I couldn't shake off these feelings. I had some lovely neighbours opposite who always checked up on me and even repaired a blown-down fence while I was at work. As they were around my parents' age, I felt slightly comforted knowing that they were there.

When the time came for the house to be sold, I started looking at houses in nearby areas and I began panicking, as I had Pepsi and didn't know what to do with him in the interim. The mortgage process was a nuisance, and as I had accumulated some debt in recent years, it took a while to find one at all! It was a year before the economic slide in 2008, so mortgage lenders weren't particularly fussy about who they lent to or the amount of money that they would lend. As a result, I was offered a mortgage at a ridiculously high interest rate for a ridiculously high amount, and I put an offer in on the first house that I viewed. The one saving grace was that I was realistic about what I could afford, and I moved a couple of miles away into an area that was unfamiliar to me. It was more of a village than a town, and I made the decision to fix the mortgage payments for five years.

I was chuffed that I'd managed to purchase a house by the age of twenty-three, and looking back, I can't believe I purchased the house at all. It was what I would call 'nursing home chic', with its pink walls, dodgy carpets and smoke-stained ceilings. The only parts of the house that appealed to me were the newly installed kitchen and the fact that the back garden was large and low maintenance. Thankfully, the only major thing I had to do was install a new central heating system; the rest was just superficial.

Around this time, I found myself with a lot of debt, which kept increasing. I was living hand-to-mouth but still trying to buy things that I couldn't afford. I kept forgetting that my friends were able to do pretty much whatever they wanted because they weren't paying a mortgage or household bills, and I tried to keep up with them. I found myself asking, 'Why did I buy this house?' And I suddenly lost my motivation to go out, or do anything really. I didn't want a housewarming party, and, other than people close to me, no one was invited to see it. I was paranoid about living on my own again, and I didn't like anyone knowing my address. Although I must say, it was the only house that I felt safe in at night.

Chapter 17

Increasing Debt

I have always been one of those impatient people who has an idea and needs to action it immediately. I couldn't wait for things or save up to ensure I could afford them; I needed to act straight away, or it would play on my mind.

The first decision I made after moving into my home was to get Pepsi a companion. I took out a payday loan and bought a Cavalier King Charles Spaniel pup for his birthday. I picked her up from a breeder around 70 miles away, and she suffered terrible travel sickness on the way back. She was tiny, and Diesel's pet carrier seemed huge compared to her. She was the cutest pup ever and looked very posh, so I named her Lady. She was a ruby Cavalier and had the pedigree name Golden Phoenix Girl issued to her by the Kennel Club. No way was I keeping that name! As was tradition, the first people to meet Lady were my grandparents, and they fell in love with her immediately.

When she and Pepsi first met, he froze, while watching her warily out of the corner of his eye, as she climbed all over him and tugged on his ears. He was such a good-natured dog I knew there was no way he would ever get vicious with her. In fact, he couldn't have been softer with her. After a couple of days, they were playing and tugging at toys together, although Pepsi always let her win. She would take bones from his mouth and settle down with them, and he never reacted or attempted to get them back. Lady and Diesel also got on well, and all three of them would spend time out in the garden playing together. After a hard day's work, I loved nothing more than cuddling up with them on the sofa – even though there was very limited space for me!

Once I had settled in, I decided to get the internal walls of the whole house replastered to have a blank canvas to decorate. I had recently been offered an 'educational experience' of a week's cruise, so I arranged for the plastering to be done during that week, and my friend stayed over to look after Pepsi, Lady and Diesel. I took out a large homeowner loan and set about paying for the plastering and organising the decorative works to be done a few weeks later. I had the entire house painted, new flooring and carpet laid throughout, replaced the lighting, and bought new furniture.

Once the loan had expired, I set up various credit cards and catalogue accounts and used them to buy more household items, both essential and non-essential, and set up the monthly finance payments. I was overstretched financially and started to feel like I was drowning. I had extremely high monthly outgoings and was having to take out payday loans each month to pay the previous one and to cover my living expenses. This was to provide for my three pets (who were also insured), pay household bills, feed myself and pay for my social life and the occasional getaway with friends.

These holidays provided an opportunity for me to relax and take a break from reality. I went away every year. They started as traditional 'girls' holidays', but over time they became relaxing breaks away with a couple of friends. I used to go clubbing in stereotypical party resorts that only seemed to encourage younger people, but ended up enjoying holidays away in nice hotels with good food, which were a distance from the main areas. My holiday spending money was solely spent on alcohol, fast food and presents for family, but as I grew up, I started spending it on things I found useful, or on activities. I remember paying a fortune one year to access the VIP lounge of a well-known nightclub, where we enjoyed unlimited drinks and socialised with the acts that were performing that evening. I barely scraped by for the last couple of days of the holiday.

It would cost a lot if I went away, as I had to pay for kennels, which were not cheap. I was also a little bit prudish and insisted on spot-checking the kennels first, paying a little more for the nicest one I could find, where the owners were fantastic, and everything was clean. Over time, the owners of these kennels became like friends, and they would treat my 'babies' like their own.

When I returned from a holiday and stepped back into the real world, the daily financial struggle simply started again. I didn't want to admit to anyone that I was struggling just yet, as I was certain I could get myself out of the mess that I had created. When it came to Christmas, I always spent way too much on everybody – as they kept telling me – but I enjoyed doing it and would get myself further and further into debt to be able to do it. I remember one year I spent solely on credit cards and added credit to my catalogue accounts to get everyone the gifts I wanted to give them.

I admitted defeat after a couple of years and opted to take out a Debt Management Plan with a charity organisation that didn't charge any fees for setting the arrangement up. This proved to be a lifesaver at the time, as it meant I had some disposable income each month. The only balances I didn't consolidate were the payday loans. Instead, I kept paying them back in full every month and then I would take out another the following month for a higher amount. I knew this couldn't go on, even with the salaries and commissions I was getting for both jobs, but I tried to hold on for as long as I could.

Chapter 18

As Useful As A One-Handed Clap...

I was struggling more and more, which only increased my anxiety, and I felt myself falling down the 'black hole' once again. I believed there was no point in life, and I assessed whether anyone would genuinely miss me. Once again, the deciding factor in staying to fight another day came from never wanting to upset anybody. I couldn't deal with the thought of my parents or grandparents blaming themselves for *my* thoughts. I also had my four-legged children to worry about now, and there was no way I could leave them behind.

I was working more and more, and my time was stretched to the point that I barely had time to pop in to see my mum. I was working all the hours offered to me and had barely any rest or time for myself. When I was at home, I was trying to tire the dogs out and making sure they were fed and watered before tending to myself. I didn't have proper meals and would just grab something from the fridge or order a takeout from the Chinese down the road. I was stressing constantly and soon developed insomnia. This was the most frustrating problem I had ever encountered. My body and mind were shattered, but the minute I tried to go to sleep, I would be wide awake, and nothing could stop the negative thoughts running through my head. I would try to grab the odd catnap on the sofa, but, with work, this was virtually impossible.

I went to see my doctor, who prescribed me sleeping tablets, with the caveat of only taking them when essential, as they were highly addictive. He also offered me anti-depressants, but as I deemed this to be embarrassing at the time, I didn't accept. The sleeping tablets were a godsend. Even though it didn't feel like I had slept, I had, and I knew my body was repairing itself, and I was more alert in the daytime. I didn't take the tablets every day, as I was conscious of the doctor's warning, but I think it made me feel better just knowing that I had them nearby. I took them 3–4 times a week for a couple of months, but then they were withdrawn to make sure I didn't have any lasting effects.

I truly felt like I had fallen down a black hole, never to return to a normal life. I had possibly never felt so low as I did in the first couple of years of becoming a homeowner. I decided I didn't like the area I had moved to and therefore hated my house. I didn't have any disposable money, and the debts were climbing every month. I had convinced myself that I could do everything, and I had a big problem with admitting that I had failed. I felt like the world's biggest failure. Everyone around me appeared to be doing well, so why wasn't I?

During this time, Pepsi had started having some behaviour problems, one of which was toileting in the house. I think he was expressing his unhappiness by being cooped up at home most of the day, and this really upset me. I didn't know what to do. I ignored the problem for longer than I should have and tried looking for any other ways to correct this behaviour, even taking him to the vet's. Then came the day I knew was coming – the day I faced facts and stopped being so selfish, putting my feelings before his happiness. I loved him so much, and this was the hardest situation I'd ever had to deal with.

Someone who worked with my mum got in touch to say their mum would love to have him. She was a fit and healthy retiree and lived right next to Bournemouth beach. I knew this would be the kindest option and that he would love it there, so I arranged for her and her husband to come and meet him. It was possibly the worst day of my life up to that point. The couple came to meet Pepsi, he showed off his tricks and his obedience, and they loved him. They arranged to come back the following week to take him to Bournemouth. It was the longest week of my life. So I made as much fuss of Pepsi as I could and tried to explain to him what was happening and the reasons behind it. Obviously, I knew he had no idea what I was prattling on about, but it made me feel better.

When the day came for him to leave, I sat outside in the back garden with Lady, and my stepdad kindly came up to hand him over to his new owners. I had packed his belongings and written a note to advise them of his diet, his microchip details, likes/dislikes, favourite toys, and anything else that I thought might be useful to know. As he was driven away, my heart broke!

Chapter 19

Escaping Debt & Health Worries

It was a few months later that my current workplace offered the option of voluntary redundancy. As I had been there for six and a half years, it was a very good offer indeed. After thinking it through, I decided to apply for it and told my parents of my decision. They were worried about me doing this, as I had been in a secure and well-paid job, but when I outlined how I could pay off my debts and give up the second job, they were supportive of my application.

Just before applying for redundancy, I had started having weird sensations in my chest, hot flushes, and losing weight. On a routine check-up with my GP, he referred me for an X-ray to rule out anything sinister and to check if there were any obvious signs why I would be experiencing these symptoms. The X-ray results came back, and I was told they had found a shadow on my lungs and a CT scan had been arranged for me to attend the following week. I was obviously nervous about the scan, and worried about the potential outcomes, but not as much as my family. (It's funny how when things are happening to you, you reassure everyone and are perfectly rational, but when it's happening to someone else, you react in a completely different manner.)

My scan results came back, and I had an appointment with a consultant, who advised that I had a mass on my lungs and Hodgkin lymphoma could be a potential diagnosis. I was referred for a bronchoscopy soon after, which is when they put a camera up your nose and down the back of your throat. This was an unpleasant experience, especially as the sedative didn't work, but as they had the live footage on a screen in front of me, it suddenly became interesting to watch.

When I went for the results a few days later, they confirmed that they could still not determine what the mass was, and so it was arranged for me to have a tracheotomy so that they could do a biopsy on the mass. I remember my mum accompanying me to my appointments with the consultant and telling her how reassured she felt while I was under her care. Her reply to my mum was that she hoped she never saw us again, as she was the 'bad news doctor'.

A short while later, my redundancy application was accepted. I was given an 'exit' date by which I would need to leave my employment, and the monies would be paid to me a week later. This was extremely exciting news. It gave me such a feeling of relief, as I saw this as the turning point in my life where things would get better, and I would be freed from the financial chains that were weighing me down. I was so lucky to be given this opportunity just when I needed it and swore never to make the same mistakes again.

I set about looking for a job to cover my monthly bills once I had left. I found one straight away with a law firm. It wasn't the best salary, but it was convenient and paved the way for me to progress. The best part was that the start date was around six weeks after leaving my job, and the tracheotomy surgery had been scheduled for the Monday following my end date, which meant I didn't need to take any time off from work. Bonus!

I had to go into hospital the night before, and I felt like a fraud sharing a ward with older, poorly people when I felt fine. At least it gave my parents and me something to chuckle about. The morning of the surgery arrived, and the only thing I was worried about was taking my tongue stud out and it still fitting after surgery. I went into theatre early, and when I woke, my parents were at my bedside looking a bit shell-shocked. I had an oxygen mask and a morphine drip going into my arm and a wad of bandaging around my throat with blood seeping through – so I imagine I did look a fright. But I felt okay. I remember having a dry throat and asking for some water and then laughing that I was like the character from *Scrooged* who has a drink and it pours out of his throat. (This was genuinely a moderate concern for the first couple of days.) But the most important thing was… my tongue stud went back in fine!

After a few hours, boredom crept in, so I got out of bed, dressed, and announced I was going home. The nurse told me that I needed to stay in overnight, but I asked them to persuade a doctor to sign me out of the hospital, as there was no way I could stay the night there, especially as I felt relatively normal. I came home and suddenly felt really self-conscious and I didn't want to go out in public for a while.

A few days later, I was able to remove the bandages and could see I had a cut across my throat (which eventually became a scar), and it made me very paranoid. I remember going out for a drink one evening and someone asked me if I'd been slashed. That's the type of comment that would usually bemuse me, and, while I laughed and said something sarcastic in response, for some reason it really got to me. A few weeks later, a friend and I had already booked to go abroad, and I was desperately applying cream to the injury in the hope that it would calm down and not be so obvious.

I was still waiting for the results of the biopsy, and after hours of trying to get answers over the telephone, my dad finally got through to the consultant, who agreed to call me. I nervously awaited his call, and it was a relief when he confirmed it was not cancerous and was a condition named sarcoidosis. He described this to me as the 'no-naming disease' (in my case), where they couldn't attribute the mass to anything else, but it wasn't cancerous. Luckily, it didn't warrant any medication, and I just needed to attend regular check-ups and undergo regular lung function tests. Finally, we'd got the result that we wanted. And I got to go on holiday with no worries, plenty of cash and ten days of lazing about in the sun with no alarm clocks waking me up for work!

Chapter 20

Searching For The Right Job
(And Finding My Wife On The Way)

I started my new job, which sounded interesting at the outset but turned out to be the complete opposite! It was working in a conveyancing branch, basically answering calls, telephoning customers with unwelcome news, filing, and logging the post – certainly *not* what had been described to me. I stuck it out for a couple of months while desperately looking for something else, when a friend told me that she knew of a job opening in her husband's workplace. I was lucky enough to secure the job, and I started working for an online retail site. I enjoyed this much more, and the team I worked with were really friendly.

While I preferred this job to the previous one, I still felt restless and found myself needing to be challenged more. So, I started looking online again. I applied for a role that involved working shifts covering a 24-hour period. This wasn't what had appealed to me, but it sounded like a challenge and the salary was better than what I was currently getting. I attended the (long) interview and nervously waited for the phone call to tell me if I was successful. A few days later, my phone rang, and I was informed that I had been successful.

I was excited to start the new role and looked forward to the new challenge.

I was finally in a better place and started to enjoy my life. I had great friends, my family was healthy, I had a job that I liked, and best of all, I had no payday loans! I had a great social life and my partner-in-crime and I were often out for drinks, the cinema, meals, whatever really. I would also meet up with workmates for drinks and had a couple of different groups of friends whom I would meet up with. There was no excuse to feel down, or so I thought, but I was. I couldn't shake off the feeling of loneliness, and I spent many evenings feeling sad and cuddling up to Lady.

I decided to buy another dog – a Cavachon named Milo. I had two reasons for getting another dog – the first being a selfish reason (he was just soooo cute), and the second reason was that I wanted Lady to have company when I wasn't at home. He was such a gorgeous dog with lots of energy, and, as he was small, his playfulness was manageable. He also loved nothing more than cuddling up to Lady and me. In fact, he used to annoy Lady, as he constantly followed her around to lie next to her.

It seemed odd that I still felt depressed, especially knowing how lucky I was in comparison to others. Maybe that was the reason why I didn't tell anyone. I felt embarrassed to feel this way, and would prefer to 'put on a brave face' and joke around as though I didn't have a care in the world. I think the 'boredom bug' had got to me again, and while I didn't have anything specific to worry about, I thought too much and dwelt on the past. I also couldn't stand to be in the house anymore. I was definitely an overthinker, and this has never boded well for me.

After a few years of working shifts, I decided that I needed to move on and settle in a permanent daytime role elsewhere, but before I had a chance to start looking properly, I suddenly developed a crippling pain in my back.

Chapter 21

More Surgery

When I first started experiencing back problems, I put it down to a sprain or injury and took some time off work to rest up. The pain didn't subside, so I went to the doctor's for some medication to help me get back on my feet. It worked for a short while, but some of the side effects made me sleepy, so there were certain times I couldn't take them.

After a couple of months, I was referred for a CT scan, which showed that a disc in my lumbar region was protruding and resting on a nerve. The solution was to have a microdiscectomy. Before considering surgery, I was encouraged to have an epidural steroid injection in my back to ease the pain. Wow! It hurt! I didn't think I would feel anything with the local anaesthetic they had administered first. I told the consultant about the pain, and he told me to be patient and see how I felt in a few days.

A few days later, the pain was just as bad as before. The side effects of the back pain far outweighed the actual pain itself, as the medication made me feel very sleepy and nauseous, so I couldn't maintain the social life I wanted. This resulted in me staying indoors a lot more, alone with my thoughts. I think even my babies were getting sick of me!

It was around this time that I met the person who later became my wife. I had never been in a same-sex relationship before, and I found the idea a little scary at the start. I worried about telling people and what they may think, and I kept our relationship a secret for a while. Turns out, I had no need to worry, as everyone was fully supportive and just glad that I was happy.

The relationship was quite tumultuous at the start, due to me wanting to keep it a secret from my friends and family. There was little trust, and I was undecided about whether to pursue it or not. I was worried about my history of getting bored easily, and I didn't want to announce this lifestyle change if it wasn't going to lead anywhere. I remember telling my best friend, to gauge her reaction, and, other than surprise, she was behind me one hundred per cent. I then told my mum and asked her to inform the family (I chickened out). They thought it 'made complete sense', seeing as I'd always very quickly got very bored with ex-partners and had never been comfortable enough with anyone to settle down.

Over time, the relationship grew stronger as I became more open about it with those around me. The initial secrecy and uncertainty gave way to trust and commitment. My friends and family were supportive, which made a significant difference. I realised that my previous fears of getting bored were unfounded, as I found a deeper connection and comfort in this relationship than I had ever experienced before.

A little while later, I was told I was on the list for surgery. I had a combination of good days and bad days, but with stronger medications, I was able to resume a 'normal-ish' life. I was frustrated to find that I could no longer wear high heels on a night out, as I was very unsteady, and my right leg would suddenly give way. I remember falling down the stairs leading to the toilet area in a nightclub. Thankfully, no damage was done, but it did end my night out, as I didn't trust myself to walk safely (especially after cocktails). Luckily, I have an amazing friend who always stayed close to me and made sure I was alright.

The surgery date I was given was about eight months later, and I found myself counting down the minutes. Despite the warning that there was only a 50/50 chance of the surgery working, it was a success!

I was poorly after the operation, and I was so upset not to be discharged on the same day that I blamed my mum for telling the consultant I'd been ill! At one point, I remember having a go at my dad for buying me a juice drink that I'd asked for, as it may have been that which had made me sick. I was adamant that I could get up and go to the toilet alone, to show the nurses that I could go home. I looked like a drunken fool, stumbling about in my hospital gown while using a walking frame that I had found propped next to an elderly lady's bed. I had barely come around from the anaesthetic, and I was given control of my Morphine drip, which I made good use of. My partner had come straight to the hospital, and I was explaining what my oxygen mask did – even though I had accidentally pulled out the wires and had it resting in the wrong place. The rest of that afternoon and the night were very hazy, and it's safe to say that I can't remember too much.

The next day, I was allowed home, and my partner came to pick me up. Much to my mum's dismay, I told her I was going to my own house and felt well enough to be on my own. This wasn't strictly true; I just didn't want to be any more of a burden than I felt I always had been. The bonus was that my partner offered to stay with me while I was recovering to help with the dogs, who absolutely adored her. It was a win-win situation for me, as she moved in and never left – and the surgery had been a success!

I needed spinal fusion surgery a few years later, just months before our wedding day. My initial concern had been setting off airport metal detectors with my new screws, but as the days passed, I found myself increasingly anxious about the upcoming surgery. The thought of the low-to-medium chance of success weighed heavily on my mind. I spent countless hours researching and preparing myself mentally for the procedure. Despite my fears, I knew that this surgery was my best hope for a better quality of life.

However, I needn't have worried because... the surgery was a success!

Throughout this journey, my wife, family and best friend have been an amazing source of support and have continued to be, through both the good times and the bad. For that, I will be forever grateful.

Chapter 22

A New Beginning

As the sun rose on a crisp autumn morning on my wedding day, the air was filled with a sense of renewal. The leaves, painted in hues of gold and crimson, danced gently in the breeze, symbolising the changes that were about to unfold. It was a day that marked the beginning of a new chapter in my life, one that I had been eagerly anticipating.

The journey leading up to this moment had been marked by both challenges and triumphs. Each obstacle had taught me valuable lessons, shaping me into the person I have become. The support of my loved ones had been unwavering, providing me with the strength to persevere. Their encouragement had been a beacon of hope, guiding me through the darkest of times.

As I stood at the threshold of this new beginning, I felt a mixture of excitement and apprehension. The future was uncertain, but it was also brimming with possibilities. I knew that the path ahead would not be easy, but I was ready to embrace it with open arms. The experiences of the past had equipped me with the resilience and determination needed to face whatever lay ahead.

With a deep breath, I took my first step forward, leaving behind the shadows of doubt and fear. The road ahead was long, but I was not alone. The journey was mine to make, and I was ready to write the next chapter of my story.

Afterword

Looking Forward

The pandemic was a very testing time for many, including me, and the world on lockdown brought much sadness and loneliness to my family and many others. It also highlighted the amazing deeds of many, the importance of good mental health and wellbeing and the support provided by local communities and charities.

On a positive note, it also brought about the next chapter in our lives – the start of our adoption journey and selling up and moving into our new home – with our little boy!

The one thing my wife and I always say, is how lucky we were to have our wedding just before COVID, for the whole family to get together and spend time having fun.

Overcoming challenges has always been a significant part of my journey. Each obstacle I faced taught me resilience and determination. There were times when the path seemed insurmountable, but I learnt to break down each challenge into manageable steps. With the support of my loved ones and a steadfast belief in my abilities, I was able to navigate through the toughest times. These experiences not only strengthened my character but also instilled in me a sense of confidence that I carry with me to this day.

I never know how I will feel each day and will probably always suffer with low self-esteem and wondering if I 'add any value to the world', but with the support of my amazing wife and family, I am feeling optimistic.

I no longer feel like I am 'outside, looking in'.

About the Author

From a young age, I found myself grappling with the heavy shadows of dejection, persistent self-doubt, and the difficult reality of self-harm. These struggles were deeply personal and, for the most part, invisible to those around me. Outwardly, I became adept at projecting an image of light-heartedness and normalcy—using humour as a shield, a way to deflect attention from the pain I carried inside. Even those closest to me rarely glimpsed the turmoil beneath the surface, as I became skilled at concealing my true feelings behind a carefully constructed mask.

For many years, I equated silence with resilience. I believed that keeping my struggles hidden was a sign of strength, that enduring quietly was somehow noble. But over time, I've come to realise that real strength is found not in isolation, but in vulnerability. It takes far more courage to be honest about one's pain, to open up and share those experiences, than it does to keep them locked away. True connection and healing begin when we allow ourselves to be seen as we truly are.

By sharing my story, I hope to illuminate the often-unspoken realities that so many people face. My intention is to foster understanding and to encourage conversations rooted in empathy and compassion. If my words help even a single person feel recognised, less alone, or empowered to seek support, then I will consider this book a success.

L J Howells

www.ingramcontent.com/pod-product-compliance
Lightning Source LLC
Chambersburg PA
CBHW051841040426
42447CB00006B/641